The Lost Art of Perseverance

Rediscover God's Perspective on Your Trials

www.graceplaceredding.com

Contributing authors: Austin Chappell, Downing McDade, Eric Heinrichs, Katherine Marx, Elizabeth Newton, Jonathan Carter

ISBN: 978-1-7321660-9-7

Preface

Perseverance is a lost art. When I first began preaching about perseverance, I had just come out of an unusually challenging season. Some of my relationships with those I trusted and thought were for me were tested significantly, and it felt like everything that could go wrong, went wrong. At certain points, I thought I might need to temporarily shut my ministry and business down. It seemed as if everything I had built with the Lord was being shaken and tried, and at times, it was all I could do to hold on and pray. It was during that time that the Lord taught me about the power of perseverance and how vital it is to keep going when we are in the midst of trials.

Little did I know that the entire world was about to enter into a season where trust would be tested more than ever. Economic shutdowns, churches choosing between meeting online and risking being closed down or having their pastors imprisoned, extreme political and social unrest, revolts, wars and rumors of wars, and collective uncertainty.

For years a large part of the Western Church has been asleep, gradually sliding back into an image that resembles the world and its systems. We have gotten very comfortable with being comfortable. Now, more than ever, we are confronted with the question, "How will we live when the very core of our faith is tested?" Amidst numerous difficulties worldwide, we have the beautiful opportunity to follow the Lord even while surrounded by opposition.

What many don't understand is that opposition carries opportunity. It's in the pressure of adverse situations that radical and exponential growth can occur. People in the world are broken and disillusioned because the systems they've relied upon and the way of life they've been used to is crumbling around them. More than ever, the Church is positioned to answer the call to the world's cries. Jesus is preparing His Bride to be radiant with His glory and effective in bringing transformation to a hurting and confused world.

For years, there have been prophetic words and murmurings of a great move of God like we have never seen before. Something big is undoubtedly coming very soon. However, the Church as a whole is not ready and God doesn't want to bring us into something we're unprepared for. He has plans and promises to fulfill in our lives that we haven't even dreamt of. This current season is merely the training ground for what's to come. God wants to take us farther, but we first need to be postured for Him to take us there. We are being refined in the fire of challenges that will make us strong enough to carry out His purposes.

At the end of my challenging season, I was able to look back and see that God had tremendously prepared me to not just overcome the difficulties set before me, but also to inspire, encourage, and raise up others to do the same. Some relationships that were tested ended up closer and stronger than before. The ministry grew in influence worldwide and has developed into something even greater.

The entire time I was going through this, the thing that kept me grounded was holding onto the Word of God and the promises He had given me. Keeping God's ultimate vision at the forefront of our minds is a key to staying encouraged when challenges come. If you have been walking through a hard season, God wants to empower you to persevere in His strength.

In Christ, we have been given the power to stand up in the middle of any trial and come out victorious.

As you read this book, I pray that the stories and teachings would renew your perspective to see through God's eyes so that you can discover and embrace *The Lost Art of Perseverance.*

Count it All Joy

Resistance makes us stronger. When we lift weights, our muscles don't just magically "get bigger." They break down, tear, and become weaker. As we recover from the damage, however, our body experiences something called "hypertrophy." This is when our muscles recover with more definition and strength than before. Just like in weightlifting, resistance is a stepping stone into greater strength. If we never face resistance, we will never reach our potential.

In this season, there is a lot of resistance against the Body of Christ. If we embrace it, it will make us stronger as we carry out the impending move of God. When we see trials how God sees them, we can see beyond the circumstances to the harvest on the other side.

God has great plans for each and every one of us. He is masterfully weaving His presence in and through our lives to establish His Kingdom upon the earth. However, we need to reach spiritual "hypertrophy" in order to stand under the weight of His calling.

You can't give children weights designed for bodybuilders and expect them to be able to lift them. In our current state of immaturity, we need to allow Christ to develop us into the fullness of His stature. I truly believe that one of the greatest moves of God is about to happen. However, we are not in the position to steward what's coming because many of us have failed to properly assess and utilize resistance. Remember, opposition carries opportunity. We need to endure and grow in the face of adversity, because it will prepare us for where God is taking us.

How many times have you found yourself in a situation that you just couldn't seem to get out of? No matter what you tried, nothing seemed to change or improve? In those times, it can be easy to get overwhelmed and forget what God is doing and saying. However, so often, the key to remaining in God's truth is not getting out of your circumstance but choosing to see it the way God does. We are limited by what we see if we look through our natural eyes. But if we look through His eyes, we will be renewed and encouraged to persevere.

If we've been relying on our own strength and motivation in times of trial, it's tempting to give up. However, that's because we are relying on ourselves instead of Him! How do we change this? It's the simple adjustment of where we put our focus.

When you are facing hard times, where are you looking? Do you look to Him who is the author and finisher of our faith? Or do you look to your own abilities? Perseverance is all about where you put your focus. Your faith will mirror what you behold. If you're focusing on yourself, you will always be self-dependent, relying on human flesh to get you through trials. However, if you focus on the love of Jesus Christ, you will be empowered by His presence, His strength, and His grace to endure.

Scripture tells us how God sees trials. He uses everything we go through to mold our character for the next season. In James 1:2-4, we learn how God wants us to see trials, "My brethren, count it all joy when you fall into various trials, knowing that the testing of your faith produces patience. But let patience have its perfect work, that you may be perfect and complete, lacking nothing."

We read this last verse and easily get encouraged, thinking "I want to be perfect, complete, and lacking nothing!" But do you realize what you just signed up for? The first step in getting to the place where you are complete and lacking nothing is letting patience have "its perfect work." This comes through the testing of your faith. It comes through choosing to "count it all joy."

Counting means adding up. Many of us look at individual moments and circumstances, but God looks at the bigger picture. When we look at an individual negative circumstance as the indication of where our future is headed, discouragement is bound to creep in. However, one trial or struggle is not indicative of where we are in Christ or what He has planned for us. When you count, you are examining your current circumstance in light of the bigger picture, like this:

My current situation + that situation of rejection + this situation of resistance + this situation of disappointment + God's words for my life = endurance

When you add up all the circumstances and see how God is using them for good, you will see how they produce joy. You start to see the big picture of what's being produced in your life as a result. We get consumed by one circumstance, making a conclusion about our entire life based on it. We get self-focused and overwhelmed, seeing that we don't have what it takes. Maybe it's a family hardship, a financial crisis, or a missed opportunity. We get focused on each individual circumstance instead of looking at the bigger picture of all these things added together.

How many of you, at some point in your life, thought something crazy was going to happen that would end the world? But guess what? You're still here. It never happened! However, many people can get so wrapped up in the fear of the moment that they forget to live in the faith of the Eternal One. Instead of getting pulled down into these circumstances as the world does, we can transcend any and every issue by *counting it all joy.*

When hard times come, whose report will you believe? The enemy, the world, the news, your doctor, those close to you, your rational mind... or will you believe the report of the Lord? You have the choice between being consumed by the way things immediately appear or choosing to set your mind on things above, where Christ is seated (Colossians 2:2).

Often, we get so frazzled when things come up because we are not fully surrendered to God. We asked Him to be our Savior, but we don't trust Him enough to be Lord. We allow Him to give us the "car" of salvation, but we demand that we drive. We put Him in the backseat as we recklessly lose sight of His heavenly perspective and purpose for our lives. This happens all the time!

In The Passion Translation, James 1:2 reads, "My fellow believers, when it seems as though you are facing nothing but difficulties, see it as an invaluable opportunity to experience the greatest joy that you can!" We should get excited whenever something bad happens. I was talking with someone about a really tough time in their life, and they told me, "It was the hardest time of my life, but I wouldn't trade it for anything. I grew and came out more mature because of it." Now that's a heavenly mindset! If we all had that mindset when opposition came our way, life would be different.

As we choose to take on this perspective, we will see our lives as a process that God is overseeing. While He is not the author of bad things, He refuses to let any bad thing go to waste because they have great potential to form strength and patience inside of us.

The Word of God says that He has plans to prosper us and not to harm us (see Jeremiah 29:11). If we choose to elevate a single negative circumstance or a series of setbacks that seem to drag us down, we can make conclusions about God's character and nature that are incorrect. We may be tempted to assume that God is not taking care of us, that we missed His will somewhere along the way, or that He has given up on us. But when we choose to see through His eyes and count it all joy, we can see His ultimate plan to prosper us no matter what we go through.

Although hard times come and our circumstances can be up and down, our conviction about God's nature and the reliability of His Word can never be shaken. We must persist in faith that all things work together for good knowing that God isn't the author of bad things. His goodness and love for us are revealed in that He uses hard times for our good if we will allow Him to form patience in us.

The temptation to give up is always there when we're going through a difficult time. I find myself being encouraged by Romans 8:28 which says "And we know that all things work together for good to those who love God, to those who are called according to His purpose." When you know that you have been made righteous, new, and are called by Him for great things, there is only one conclusion to make about the trying difficulty you are facing: if it's not good yet, then God's not done! Despite what many in the world believe, God certainly is not the one who is causing the bad things to happen in your life to punish you for the wrong you have done. When you came to Christ, all of your sins and the punishment due to you were forgiven in Him. God isn't sending bad situations into your life, but He is certainly going to use the trying times to perfect Himself in you so He can work everything together for your good. Instead of being discouraged in hard circumstances, be encouraged because something good is going to come from it.

When you travel as much as I do, the chance of something going wrong with your trip is highly likely. I can't tell you how many times my luggage has been lost or damaged, leaving me without clothes, toiletries, and other necessities. It would be easy to get frustrated by not having the things I need, but I've grown to be excited because I know that something good is always coming on the other side. I tell my leadership team that this concept is called "inconvenient favor." It's when something inconvenient happens that turns out for good. I once traveled for a wedding, and the airline lost my bag with my suit, so I was compensated with a completely new suit and it was nicer than the one that they had lost. On top of all of that, the bag ended up returning to me later with all of my possessions! If the circumstances around you have not turned out for good, then God is not done working in your life. Pastor Charles Swindoll once said, "Life is 10% what happens to you and 90% how you react to it." When you change your perspective on trials, you'll change the whole experience you have with your issues.

One of the biggest perspective shifts we can make is getting our eyes off of ourselves and onto Jesus. Today's culture has majored in the opposite! God wants us to put the focus back on Him. Let me illustrate by using this scripture:

> Now to Him who is able to do exceedingly abundantly above all that we ask or think, according to the power that works in us, to Him be glory in the church by Christ Jesus to all generations, forever and ever. Amen.
>
> —Ephesians 3:20-21

Think about it. What's one of the biggest reasons we don't fulfill the call of God on our lives? It's us. Our pride, our fear, our mistakes, and our issues. Our reasoning for failing is all about "Me, me, me." Ephesians 3:20, however, does not say, "Now unto ME that is able..." It says, "Now unto HIM that is able." You are not able to fulfill the call of God on your life. If you can do what God has called you to do all by yourself, then you probably don't understand what He's called you to. That's the whole point of the Gospel—you can't do it on your own.

If we believe it's up to our own human flesh to walk like Christ, then we will excuse and rationalize everything including our sin and compromise. Have you ever heard the phrase, "There's grace for that"? Someone sins and then they dismiss it with, "Well there's grace for that, brother." NO! That's a slap in the face of what Jesus did. Grace is not a license to sin.

In fact, Titus 2:11-12 says, "For the grace of God that brings salvation has appeared to all men, teaching us that, denying ungodliness and worldly lusts, we should live soberly, righteously, and godly in the present age..." Grace does not excuse our sin, but it instructs us to deny all ungodliness!

When people say "there's grace for that," it shows they don't even know what grace is! Paul himself said that sin no longer has dominion over him because he's no longer under the law but under grace. So when someone is in sin, they're not in grace at all. They don't need grace; they need mercy. Grace is getting something you don't deserve. Mercy is *not* getting what you *do* deserve. You deserve punishment for sin, but Jesus took the punishment and extended mercy to you.

When you receive grace, there's an empowerment that comes that allows you to deny ungodliness and live a life that's holy and set apart. Grace itself allows for the power of God to flow through you. It gets your eyes off of yourself! You stop looking at your weakness, sin, and shortcomings and turn to focus on Jesus' ability, kindness, and mercy. When grace is present in your life, the power of God will be present as well. When His power is present in your life, you'll be able to push through any difficulty you face.

On one recent trip, I was scrolling through the classic movies on the airplane and realized that they don't make movies like those anymore! Main characters in titles like *Rocky*, *Remember the Titans*, and *The Karate Kid* all had a coach pushing them forward and calling them into unforeseen potential. Quitting wasn't an option. It was always about persevering into the seemingly impossible!

I have been discipling people for decades now, and I have learned that one of my biggest mistakes when learning to father and lead young adults has been babying them. Often I would feel sorry when someone was going through a difficult time, and I pulled them out of the "fire" too quickly. This is a common mistake leaders make because we love people and do not want them to suffer! But just because we may be able to bail someone out of a hard situation does not mean we should. We could be interrupting something God wants to form inside of them as a result of enduring that circumstance.

When Moses led the Israelites out of Egypt, they had a remarkably short memory while wandering through the desert. They were freed from centuries of brutal slavery to one of the largest and most dominating empires of all time. They had lost their identity as an independent nation and were not living in God's design for them as His chosen people. In the process of being led back to the promised land given to their honored father, Abraham, they did not eagerly expect the abundance that would be there for them. Instead, they looked around at the dry ground on the way and were distracted by the lack they saw. In their hunger, they whined, "It would have been better that we died in Egypt!" (see Exodus 16:2-3).

The same attitude arises when we condition people to believe that they don't have to endure challenges in the process of fulfilling their purpose. If we relieve the pressure they are feeling by removing the trial, they will get discouraged in future circumstances instead of being made stronger through perseverance. When we go through a hard time and that season ends, there is a rewarding moment of thankfulness when we see how God used it to shape us and make us stronger. This motivates us to persevere the next time we go through a difficult season.

Think of the generals of the faith that you admire. I've been privileged to sit with many generals and hear their stories. They have gone through so much persecution and difficulty, all to follow what God was doing and preach the simple Gospel. Through numerous difficulties, they discovered the lost art of persevering in the Word of the Lord and His promises. We have to ask ourselves, "How would we like to go through what they went through?"

It's not just the generals of today. The Bible itself is full of stories of men and women that we admire for their perseverance. They went before us and set inspiring examples of radical lives lived in submission to God. But it can be easy to see the fruit of their lives without first seeing the trials and challenges they went through. In reality, these were not superheroes that were especially gifted. They were ordinary men and women, just like us, who went through hard times of their own.

If we acknowledged the hard times these people went through in light of where God ultimately brought them, we wouldn't get discouraged when we hit hard times. If we saw what they went through, we would have a proper perspective allowing us to persist through hardship and difficulty. We would run at problems and destroy them instead of running from them because we would be convinced that God would use it to form and shape character within us. God is raising us up to be champions. Champions eat problems for breakfast.

According to Romans 8:37, we are more than overcomers, not "run-from-ers." We have to shift our mindset about the problems we face. When challenges come up, we've got to think, "Okay, I'm going to destroy this thing!" You are not less than the problems you face. You've got the Spirit of all truth living in you who loves leading you into truth. That means there's not a problem coming at you that you can't solve. Whether it's natural or supernatural, you've got access to the solution.

I believe there will be an impartation through these pages for you to continue in perseverance no matter what you are facing. God is going to seal in your heart the calling He has placed on your life. He is going to fill you with His presence so you will know you are not alone. He wants to set your sights higher so nothing will be able to discourage you. It won't matter what else comes against you—you will be marked for Him, and His grace will keep you and preserve you. God's presence is alive today to awaken perseverance in His Church, that we would endure and come out on the other side as mature sons and daughters.

I believe that we're about to enter into a season of maturity like we've never seen before. In the process of entering into that season, we will be able to walk out the Great Commission in a way that we've never experienced before.

As you're reading this book, God is going to impart to you more hope, momentum, drive, and endurance than you've ever had before.

No Compromise

Any test of perseverance brings character if we choose to let it. If we fail to see what God is doing through hard times, we will miss out on what He wants to build in us. Don't be so focused on one moment that you lose sight of the big picture. It's all joy from God's perspective. See hard times as opportunities to develop character, and you will persevere through all things, confident that they are working for your good.

We are often very focused on pleasure and feeling good. We've made it all about our "hearts" and emotions. But where does the truth come into this? What about transcending above our circumstances and the emotions they provoke? As I stated earlier, we value so many greats of the faith but we forget what they went through to get to where God brought them. God is far more interested in the process than the destination. The only way you'll enter your potential is by persevering in the midst of problems and pain.

In this chapter, we're going to spend a lot of time looking at Daniel 3, where Shadrach, Meshach, and Abednego were presented with a really big problem. First, these three men were the property of a foreign king who had conquered their homeland and taken them captive. They had been chosen to serve in the king's court because of their looks, intellect, and wisdom. The king they had been selected to serve was an evil, self-seeking, and narcissistic man.

Desiring even more worship and adoration than he already had, Nebuchadnezzar constructed a giant golden image of himself and demanded that all the people of Babylon bow down to worship it multiple times a day. In other words, he was saying, "bow down and worship *me* as your god."

Sometimes when I share this story in the Western World, people reply with, "Ah, but Daniel, we don't worship idols in the West today though. That's only for those people in Asia and Africa." Don't be so sure. While not many of us in Western civilization keep golden images we bow down to, we do very often worship success, money, fame, influence, technological advancement, moral superiority, etc. *Anything* that takes the place of God in your life is an idol and needs to be torn down. With that, let's look again at the story of Daniel's friends.

Anyone in Babylon who refused to bow down would evoke the wrath of the king and be sentenced to death by fire in a giant furnace. Shadrach, Meshach, and Abednego, who faithfully worshipped the God of Israel only, were given a choice: bow down or go in the furnace.

How would we handle that situation today? When given the choice between your convictions and living to see tomorrow, what would you choose? For Shadrach, Meshach, and Abednego, the choice seemed obvious. There doesn't appear to be a hint of hesitation or doubt in their story. They had already made up their minds.

> O Nebuchadnezzar, we have no need to answer you in this matter. If that is the case, our God whom we serve is able to deliver us from the burning fiery furnace, and He will deliver us from your hand, O king. But if not, let it be known to you, O king, that we do not serve your gods, nor will we worship the gold image which you have set up.
>
> —Daniel 3:16-18

Read that Scripture again. What did they say? *"Even if God doesn't* deliver us, we will not bow to you." Now *that* is perseverance. If we are only Christians for the moments of deliverance, the freedom, and the blessings, we will crumble in the face of persecution. We don't persevere just so we can be set free—we persevere because we refuse to compromise on what and *who* we believe in. It's about choosing God no matter what comes our way, even if it costs us our lives.

However, the sad reality is that most of us have already bowed to much less than a "Nebuchadnezzar." We bow to emotions, fleeting feelings, and flat tires. Many of us would have looked at Nebuchadnezzar and said:

"Um... king, I don't really have peace about this right now. That furnace feels really hot to me. Could you maybe make it a little cooler, so it doesn't hurt as much when I go in?" "What if I bowed down maybe just a little bit? Or only bow down some days, but not every day?" "I mean, as long as I'm not bowing down in my heart, it doesn't really matter what I do with my body, right?"

Shadrach, Meshach, and Abednego didn't justify the situation. They faced it head on. Their answer was plain and simple: "Do what you want to us. We're not bowing down. Try to kill us if you want to. We're not even sure you'll be able to, but you're welcome to try." They lived a life of absolutely no compromise. Bowing was not an option. The slightest compromise wasn't of interest. It didn't matter the circumstances or how hard the king could make life for them. Standing in faithfulness was worth whatever price they had to pay. They were so grounded in their trust in God that they were willing to say, "King, we will not bow."

> Then Nebuchadnezzar was full of fury, and the expression on his face changed toward Shadrach, Meshach, and Abed-Nego. He spoke and commanded that they heat the furnace seven times more than it was usually heated. And he commanded certain mighty men of valor who were in his army to bind Shadrach,

> Meshach, and Abed-Nego, and cast them into the burning fiery furnace. Then these men were bound in their coats, their trousers, their turbans, and their other garments, and were cast into the midst of the burning fiery furnace.
>
> —Daniel 3:19-21

Think about this: Shadrach, Meshach, and Abednego's decisions made things *worse* for them. Their course of action put them in direct opposition to the ruling authority. What happens when you make a decision that makes life harder for yourself? What do you do when you have to make a decision that you know is going to *cause* you to be attacked?

You may be thinking to yourself, "I have done this whole resistance thing before, and it's one thing to resist *one* time. But when you are being attacked again and again, it gets more and more difficult to endure." What if I have to *keep* enduring and *keep* resisting? More than ever, this generation is a "now" generation. We have gotten so used to instant results and being able to access any information in a matter of seconds. Being conditioned to the "now" mentality cripples us because we assume the very presence of resistance means something is wrong. But this is not the case! In fact, resistance is often the indication that you are moving in the right direction. Sometimes the only right step to take is the one in the direction of the furnace, and the only way to see God come through is to face the fire.

> Then King Nebuchadnezzar was astonished; and he rose in haste and spoke, saying to his counselors, "Did we not cast three men bound into the midst of the fire?" They answered and said to the king, "True, O king." "Look!" he answered, "I see four men loose, walking in the midst of the fire; and they are not hurt, and the form of the fourth is like the Son of God." Then Nebuchadnezzar went near the mouth of the burning fiery furnace and spoke, saying, "Shadrach, Meshach, and Abed-Nego, servants of the Most High God, come out, and come here." Then Shadrach, Meshach,

> and Abed-Nego came from the midst of the fire. And the satraps, administrators, governors, and the king's counselors gathered together, and they saw these men on whose bodies the fire had no power; the hair of their head was not singed nor were their garments affected, and the smell of fire was not on them.
>
> —Daniel 3:24-27

How many of you know, when you have faith and you're grounded in who you are, you can walk in the midst of the fire, and nothing can burn you! Some of you are in the midst of the fire right now, but the fire can't burn you when you know who you are. Not only that, but the fire reveals who was with you the entire time. Was God with Shadrach, Meshach, and Abednego the entire time? Yes. But it wasn't until they were cast into the very heart of the fire that the glory of God was revealed for everyone else to see. The truly incredible part of this story is that Shadrach, Meshach, and Abednego's refusal to submit opened the door to their ruling authorities to an encounter with the one true God.

> Nebuchadnezzar spoke, saying, "Blessed be the God of Shadrach, Meshach, and Abed-Nego, who sent His Angel and delivered His servants who trusted in Him, and they have frustrated the king's word, and yielded their bodies, that they should not serve nor worship any god except their own God! Therefore I make a decree that any people, nation, or language which speaks anything amiss against the God of Shadrach, Meshach, and Abed-Nego shall be cut in pieces, and their houses shall be made an ash heap; because there is no other God who can deliver like this." Then the king promoted Shadrach, Meshach, and Abed-Nego in the province of Babylon.
>
> —Daniel 3:28-30

Here's the real takeaway from this story: Shadrach, Meshach, and Abednego may be the ones who were willing to face a furnace, but the story is really NOT about them! The end of the story isn't about Shadrach, Meshach, and Abednego having a better day and getting promoted (even though that does happen). The story is about God's glory! The king of a pagan nation made a decree of protection. But when we're faced with the fiery furnace, we make it about us! We think, "Oh, the pain! Oh, it's hot! My heart's just not open for that right now!" When we're in that place, we're not focused on Him. In fact, self-focus actually robs us of the ability to consider the trial we're going through with joy!

The reason Shadrach, Meshach, and Abednego's story ends with king Nebuchadnezzar glorifying God is because they chose to glorify God! They were focused on Him. Their faith was grounded and rooted in Him. Because of it, they boldly went in and said, "We're protected, but even if we're not, we're not bowing because bowing is not an option."

Your breakthrough is really not about you at all. It's about God receiving glory through you. When Nebuchadnezzar recognized the three young men, he made a decree to the entire nation acknowledging God. When God works all things for good in our lives, He is glorified. When we understand this, we will persevere to see the greatest breakthroughs we've seen in our lives and the greatest victories of our generation.

What is holding us back from seeing the breakthrough and God getting the glory through our lives? Our beliefs. Our belief system is like a dam holding back the breakthroughs we're really after. We're making it about us. We are so focused on ourselves, our financial breakthrough, our healing, our relational reconciliation, what we need or want that we've forgotten that we exist for Jesus and to make Him known. Do you want to know what happens when we make things about Jesus? He shows up. His power shows up because He sees a son or daughter whose heart is to make Him known.

Pride comes before the fall. When your desire is to making your name great, you're on your own. You will only succeed as far as your strength is able to carry you. God resists the proud, but He exalts the humble. Humility acknowledges who life is really about and who is really in control. When we go through life needing Him to show up for things to work out, He is faithful to do so.

Many of us have forgotten what perseverance looks like because we are used to getting our way instantly. As soon as we realize, "It's not going the way I wanted," then we are quick to say "this is not what I signed up for." If we were honest, what we really think is that perseverance is the process of finding a solution to our problem that sidesteps our own pain and suffering. This reveals that we have given a commitment conditional on our enjoyment of the process and not for God's purposes. We cannot afford to compromise because we stand for God and seek His ultimate glory. We are living lives of holiness and excellence for the glory of God and for His Kingdom. No moment of compromise is acceptable.

You may ask, "Well, Daniel, that's all well and good, but what if nothing ever changes? What happens if things just stay hard? When is it acceptable to give up?" Let me remind you of Shadrach, Meshach, and Abednego's conviction. They said, "Even if He does not deliver us, we still won't bow." In other words, they were okay with the possibility of not surviving the trial, never seeing the thing they were promised. That was okay. Resistance and perseverance were worth it. Knowing they never compromised by worshiping another god was worth whatever the cost they had to pay.

That's an amazing statement of faith! At the end of the day, it wasn't about what they could handle. It was about surrender to the Lord. It's in surrender that grace comes, and we can live this way too. I believe God is raising up a holy, generation without compromise that is empowered by grace to live that kind of lifestyle.

You probably know the story of Daniel and the lion's den. Daniel was a righteous man entrapped by a bunch of jealous political leaders who hated the fact that he had favor with the king. Again, they made a law saying "worship our gods or die." Daniel wouldn't. A person of compromise who doesn't value conviction might "obey the law of the land" over their relationship with the Lord. They might try to hide their faith and keep it quiet. "It would be justified, right?" they wonder, "Just appease the political and religious elites on the surface with a little bow. Why does it matter if it lets you keep your status and comfort intact?" We rationalize and justify, making things sound better, look better, and feel better than what they are. Daniel was a man of no compromise. He wasn't going to change His relationship with God because of his circumstances.

It's powerful to see how Daniel's faithfulness to the Lord moved the heart of the king. He knew he was trapped by his own words, but even so, Daniel 6 says King Darius actually *hoped* Daniel's God would deliver him! King Darius was so troubled, he spent the entire night fasting, and not allowing himself to be entertained (that's quite an extensive fast!).

> At the first light of dawn, the king got up and hurried to the lions' den. When he came near the den, he called to Daniel in an anguished voice, "Daniel, servant of the living God, has your God, whom you serve continually, been able to rescue you from the lions?" Daniel answered, "May the king live forever!"
>
> —Daniel 6:19-21 NIV

There's something about being so focused on the Lord that you don't really focus on yourself anymore. Daniel, having spent the night in what should have been a death sentence, let the first words from his mouth be a blessing toward the leader that had thrown him into the pit in the first place: *"May the king live forever!"* I hear people complain a lot about leadership in their lives. "Can you believe what this person did to me? That leader said this to me, and I just can't believe it!" Think about who some of the people in the Bible honored and served. Shadrach, Meshach, and Abednego *continued* to serve King Nebuchadnezzar after he tried to have them killed. Daniel served *many* evil kings, including Darius, who had him tossed into a pit of lions.

But that's not where their stories end. Because they persevered, God used them to bring the knowledge of God into pagan, idol-worshipping peoples. People living in darkness saw a great light.

> Then King Darius wrote to all the nations and peoples of every language in all the earth: "May you prosper greatly! "I issue a decree that in every part of my kingdom people must fear and reverence the God of Daniel. "For he is the living God and he endures forever; his kingdom will not be destroyed, his dominion will never end. He rescues and he saves; he performs signs and wonders in the heavens and on the earth. He has rescued Daniel from the power of the lions."
>
> —Daniel 6:25-27

We make things so much about ourselves that we often stop the breakthrough from blessing those around us. When Daniel was faced with his decision to persevere, it wasn't about what was best for him. It was about making God's name known throughout the earth. Every time a challenge arises, we have the ability to say, "This is about Jesus. It's not about me." When you make it about Him, you open the door and floodgates for miracles, signs, and wonders and to glorify Him.

There is a biblical principle that teaches that what you focus on, you magnify. What you give attention to, you will get more of, for good or evil. If you focus on problems, you'll get more problems. But if you focus on peace and hope, guess what you get? It's time we stop worrying about our problems and circumstances and start believing that God is with us *in* our problems and circumstances! Even more importantly, it's time we started believing that God is *bigger* than our problems and circumstances. What you magnify gets bigger! Answer the question for yourself: Do I want big problems or big solutions? How you answer that will tell you everything you need to know about where you should place your focus.

Looking Unto Him

There is great personal reward from enduring through trial and choosing to persevere. But ultimately, our lives are not about ourselves. The key to walking in the lost art of perseverance is realizing that we are not persevering in our own strength. Our entire lives are a process of learning to depend on God in everything we do, that He would be glorified through each and every moment. A great key here is being rooted in our identity in Christ, continually looking to Him. By "looking unto Jesus, the author and finisher of our faith" instead of focusing on ourselves, we allow His perspective and will to reign in our lives (Hebrews 12:2).

When we find ourselves going through a hard time, sometimes the temptation is to fail in areas of character or spiritual maturity. The enemy will try to take advantage of a time when we feel tired. He can whisper in our ear, "You've been working hard for a long time. You could use a break. You succeeded in this other area, so you can afford to compromise in this area." We could struggle with a number of lies, but we must rise up in these times and know that there is something bigger at stake than this single moment.

When life becomes difficult, we must not be short-sighted about the broader plan of God and the agenda of the enemy. God and His Kingdom are continually advancing, and the kingdom of darkness is resisting it (see Matthew 11:12). While the enemy is not to be a focus in our lives, it would be irresponsible for us to remain unaware of his attempts to derail us from God's plan. When we fail in matters of holiness or excellence, it is not just us who suffer. The kingdom of darkness stops the advancement of God's light in that area, and if we are not quick to repent, a domino effect ensues that extends beyond our own lives and to those around us.

When you are in the middle of temptation, ask yourself, "Who is to gain from this if I give in?" The lie that is being sold to you is that you will gain, but in reality, only evil gains when you settle for less than God's best for you. Now, who is to gain from the times you resist temptation? It's not only for your benefit, but for those around you. Your perseverance is all for God's glory and the advancement of His Kingdom. We are in a war, and both sides want to take ground. God's side will always prevail in the bigger picture so long as we keep our eyes fixed on Him and choose to live a life of no compromise.

It's the times of resisting temptation that make us stronger the next time we are tempted. What's the fruit? Our character is being refined! Instead of seeing temptation as failure in and of itself, we must recognize it for what it is: an opportunity to grow in resisting evil and living a life of radiant holiness in the strength of Christ. Keep this before you when you are going through temptation, and you will notice God's truth brings you life and strength to persevere.

I believe one of the biggest strongholds of the enemy in the Body of Christ is that we're becoming self-focused. God is looking to bring the focus off of us and back onto Him so that we can stand firm. Take a moment to ask yourself a serious question: "Who is the Lord of my life–me, or Jesus?" When we surrendered our lives to Christ, we gave ownership of our lives to Him! We gave up our rights. We are no longer on the throne of our lives, making the decisions. The price Jesus paid is too costly for us to take back the reins and steer our lives into compromise.

When you're faced with personal resistance, realize it's not about you. It's about the breakthrough that will come to others because of the breakthrough you chose to walk in. The victory God will win in your life is not just for your situation—it's about the other people who will hear the testimony and be encouraged to see God move in similar ways in their own lives. God's call on our lives is way bigger than we have ever dreamed. We must not become short-sighted due to self-focus.

Imagine what would have happened if David's perspective on life had been short-sighted. Would we even know his name today? Would he have been found worthy to become the founder of the kingly line from which Jesus would eventually come? In 1 Samuel 16, the prophet Samuel came to Jesse's house, asking for his sons. Jesse called up all of his sons to be there to meet the prophet... except David. David's own father forgot about him! If he were a part of the modern-day Western Church, he would be in inner healing for years! "When I was twelve, my own father forgot me and left me to take care of sheep while he and my brothers went to a party! I felt so rejected!"

Fortunately, David knew he had a Father in heaven that loved Him, and He's the one who sent the prophet! His family might have forgotten about him, but God knew exactly where he was.

> So it was, when they came, that he looked at Eliab and said, "Surely the Lord's anointed is before Him!" But the Lord said to Samuel, "Do not look at his appearance or at his physical stature, because I have refused him. For the Lord does not see as man sees; for man looks at the outward appearance, but the Lord looks at the heart." So Jesse called Abinadab, and made him pass before Samuel. And he said, "Neither has the Lord chosen this one." Then Jesse made Shammah pass by. And he said, "Neither has the Lord chosen this one." Thus Jesse made seven of his sons pass before Samuel. And Samuel said to Jesse, "The Lord has not chosen these." And Samuel said to Jesse, "Are all the young men

> here?" Then he said, "There remains yet the youngest, and there he is, keeping the sheep." And Samuel said to Jesse, "Send and bring him. For we will not sit down till he comes here." So he sent and brought him in. Now he was ruddy, with bright eyes, and good-looking. And the Lord said, "Arise, anoint him; for this is the one!" Then Samuel took the horn of oil and anointed him in the midst of his brothers; and the Spirit of the Lord came upon David from that day forward.
>
> —1 Samuel 16:6-13

Let's pause for a moment. If you are reading this book and feel like you are stuck or that you have been forgotten, God knows exactly where *you* are. Don't be intimidated or discouraged when it feels like great things are happening in the lives of people all around you, but you aren't moving. God sees you, He knows you, and He has great plans for you. Don't stop doing what you know you should be doing! Galatians 6:9 says, "Let us not grow weary while doing good, for in due season we shall reap if we do not lose heart." Just like He did with David, He can change your whole life in an instant by sending a "Samuel" to promote you.

Let's fast-forward to 1 Samuel 17, where we read about the Philistines attacking the Israelites. Every day for forty days, the armies would line up to attack each other. Every day, the attack would come to a grinding halt when the Philistine champion Goliath, a nine-foot-tall giant, would step out from the ranks and taunt the Israelites and their God. He would call for a champion from Israel to step out and fight him in winner-take-all single combat. In other words, "If I win, you're our slaves, but if you win, we'll be your slaves." For forty days, nobody came forward, not even the king.

Israel was suffering from an identity crisis. They couldn't see a way that they could ever defeat this monster of a man. They saw their own limitations, their weakness, and their inability. What they forgot to account for was God's ability. One day, David showed up to the battlefield to take lunch to his older brothers who were in the army. It was going to be a quick visit until he heard Goliath yelling out insults against his God.

David had a different way of seeing things. He had the mindset of a champion and a victor. He was deeply bothered by the words of Goliath, but not in the least bit afraid. David, this young kid from nowhere, had the boldness and audacity to ask, "What's going to happen to the man who kills Goliath?"

David's brothers were shocked and deeply offended. "Who does this David think he is to be able to do something we can't?" they wondered. They said, "Why did you come down here? And with whom have you left those few sheep in the wilderness? I know your pride and the insolence of your heart, for you have come down to see the battle" (1 Samuel 17:28).

If David were a member of most of our modern churches, he'd be crushed. "I can't believe it! Not only does my dad not believe in me, but neither do my brothers! They think I'm prideful and irresponsible!" Let me be clear that I'm not making fun of people who struggle with those kinds of thoughts. I'm just trying to show you the difference between those who struggle to rise up in their identity in Christ and those who don't. The people who don't are the ones who are grounded in faith, who understand that God is bigger than their problems. They understand that they have been co-crucified, co-buried, co-raised, and they're co-seated with Christ as co-heirs (see Romans 6:2-10). You can't know these truths and be self-focused at the same time.

> Now when the words which David spoke were heard, they reported them to Saul; and he sent for him. Then David said to Saul, "Let no man's heart fail because of him; your servant will go and fight with this Philistine."
>
> —1 Samuel 17:31-32

King Saul heard that someone in the camp was feeling brave enough to face the giant and sent for him. David's confidence in God promoted him. When you have genuine confidence and faith in God, people notice. It draws attention. The world is used to seeing self-confidence. In many ways, it's the currency of our age. But when someone displays confidence, not in their own flesh, but in the grace of God, it turns heads. Faith in God will promote you and get you to places of influence you never would have gotten if you were just believing in yourself. What you believe about God matters.

I grew up going to a Baptist Christian school and a Charismatic church. During the week, I would hear messages at school about how I was an evil, wicked sinner with nothing good in me. Then I would go to church on Sunday and I would hear things like, "You're amazing! You're a world-changer! You're going to shape history!" Most of you probably grew up on one side or the other. The thing is that both of these messages have truth in them. Before (or without) Jesus, I was an evil, wicked sinner who had nothing good in me. However, now that I'm in Christ, I am amazing! I am a world- changer! These statements are two sides of the same coin, and in the middle is Jesus on the Cross. Without Him, I'm nothing. With Him, I have everything.

We can't leave Jesus out of the equation. Only looking at one side of the coin leaves us lacking. Going through life as a Christian believing that you're still evil and wicked leads to a life filled with fear and condemnation. We must see that because we are in Christ, we have been cleansed of all wickedness and sin. On the other hand, going through life believing that you're amazing and awesome without remembering where you came from leads to pride and arrogance. The Gospel is the plumb line that keeps us centered on Jesus in our Christian walk.

We have to allow the Word to define our experience, not the other way around. Whether we are living in the experience of all of God's promises or not does not define whether His Word is true. Conversely, if it is true in the Word, then we should want it in our life. On one side are the Charismatic Christians who have experiences with the Holy Spirit and see manifestations of His glory. On the other side, are conservative Christians who strongly value the Word. The Charismatic Christian that relies heavily on the encounters that they have without having the Word as their foundation oftentimes goes into deception. The conservative Christian that relies only on their understanding of the Word and doesn't have room for the move of the Spirit often ends up in religion.

R. T. Kendall compares this tension to growing up in a divorced family. Somewhere in the Church today there has been a divorce of the Word and the Spirit. We have to allow the move of the Spirit and His Word to bring us into a place of balance. If you want to know more about living in balance, check out my devotional book *Truth In Tension: 55 Days to Living in Balance.* I would love to take the majority of the Charismatic Church and put them into conservative churches and vice versa. I have discipled people from both sides.

When I disciple someone who is strong in the Word, I challenge them to spend time in meetings where the Spirit is moving strongly. When they see someone encountering the Spirit, I encourage them not to judge what is happening by what they see, but rather to ask God and ask the person about what they are experiencing. You are not the judge of their heart intentions before the Lord. Don't put yourself in that position.

When discipling people who are strong in the moving of the Spirit but weak in the Word, I encourage them to spend more time in Scripture. I have often heard things said in Charismatic circles such as, "I don't even know what to do or where to go." The last time I checked, the Bible says, "Thy Word is a lamp unto my feet and a light unto my path" (Psalm 119:105). Or this: "Daniel, I don't know what to do–I'm struggling with sin." The Bible says, "Thy Word have I hidden in my heart that I might not sin against you" (Psalm 119:11). God doesn't need to speak to you in a vision or a dream in these situations because He has already spoken to you through His Word.

> And Saul said to David, "You are not able to go against this Philistine to fight with him; for you are a youth, and he a man of war from his youth."
>
> —1 Samuel 17:33

When Saul saw that his "champion" was a scrawny kid, he laughed. "Who does this guy think he is to face a giant?" Man! When will David catch a break? First his father, then his brothers, and now even the *king* doesn't believe in him! But I don't see David complaining about that in the story, do you? He didn't run away, cry, throw a tantrum, or go into his past to try to figure out why so many people are rejecting him. He didn't care about the opinion of any of these men. He knew God believed in him, and he was far more concerned with God's opinion of him than anyone else's. More than that, David does something incredible. He begins to tell Saul the testimony of his life.

> Your servant used to keep his father's sheep, and when a lion or a bear came and took a lamb out of the flock, I went out after it and struck it, and delivered the lamb from its mouth; and when it arose against me, I caught it by its beard, and struck and killed it. Your servant has killed both lion and bear; and this uncircumcised Philistine will be like one of them, seeing he has defied the armies of the living God.
>
> —1 Samuel 17:34-36

David, an adolescent shepherd, had more faith, confidence, and belief in God than anyone in the army of Israel. Logically speaking, any soldier in the army of Israel would have stood a better chance than this kid. But God's logic works differently than ours. Consider this: if God would have raised up someone in the army, a combat-trained soldier, what do you think would have happened? Chances are they would have attributed it to their own strength or training. It's a smaller jump to make than if you're a teenage sheepherder armed with a slingshot. David knew this was God's battle to win, but he was willing to be the vessel for victory. This way the only one who would get any glory for the victory would be God.

> So Saul clothed David with his armor, and he put a bronze helmet on his head; he also clothed him with a coat of mail. David fastened his sword to his armor and tried to walk, for he had not tested them. And David said to Saul, "I cannot walk with these, for I have not tested them." So David took them off.
>
> —1 Samuel 17:38-39

David put on Saul's armor and very quickly discovered he wouldn't be able to walk in it, much less fight a nine-foot-tall giant. Saul's armor was the best there was in Israel, and it was made specifically for him. It more than likely weighed in the ballpark of 150 pounds. For all we know David likely didn't even weigh 150 pounds!

Let me make an important point here. Saul's armor was meant for only one person: Saul. It was made to be useful for Saul's style of fighting, to fit well to his body shape, and to be supported by his frame. It was *never* made to fit David. In the same way, you are not meant to wear someone else's armor. You cannot mimic someone else's life or gifting. God made you in *His* image, not in the image of another person. You were born a completely unique original. Don't die a copy of someone else.

Oftentimes, the source of discouragement when we are going through a trial is comparison. We look at other people's prosperity and how much they are growing. Then we become focused on ourselves and think, "Why am I not getting what he has? Why can't I experience what she is experiencing?" This reveals that we are not seeing our circumstances for what they are in light of God's broader purposes. We are allowing offense to build because we are looking at ourselves in comparison to others instead of seeing ourselves in Christ.

We make things about us too much. We make prayers and worship songs about us, singing about our experiences instead of about what God has done and who He is. If we understand that God's greater view is about His Kingdom and not just about our individual lives, we would have more confidence and motivation to persevere! We would see that His purpose is to use us so that everyone would know Him. When we think it's about us, we think His power is limited because of the wrong we've done or the good we haven't done.

When we get our focus off of ourselves and put it back on Him, we're able to be encouraged and say, "God, I can't do this without you, I need you more than ever." God is wanting to ground us in faith. He is building a people that are grounded in the faith that God is bigger than their issues and their problems. It's self-focus that leads to identity issues, in either extreme of pride or in low self-worth. The key to remaining balanced is focusing on Jesus.

The enemy has gotten us so deceived by self-focus that whenever something doesn't look good, feel good, or sound good, we think, "Oh, well, I'm tired of this. I'm moving on to the next thing." And we quit. But God is looking for people who have perseverance and endurance to walk this thing out while living a life of no compromise.

> So the Philistine said to David, "Am I a dog, that you come to me with sticks?" And the Philistine cursed David by his gods. And the Philistine said to David, "Come to me, and I will give your flesh to the birds of the air and the beasts of the field!" Then David said to the Philistine, "You come to me with a sword, with a spear, and with a javelin. But I come to you in the name of the Lord of hosts, the God of the armies of Israel, whom you have defied. This day

> the Lord will deliver you into my hand, and I will strike you and take your head from you. And this day I will give the carcasses of the camp of the Philistines to the birds of the air and the wild beasts of the earth, that all the earth may know that there is a God in Israel. Then all this assembly shall know that the Lord does not save with sword and spear; for the battle is the Lord's, and He will give you into our hands."
>
> —1 Samuel 17:44-47

Courage is not the absence of fear. Courage is the decision to push through fear, acting on what is right regardless of how you feel. It's the ability to look beyond the thing that stands immediately in your way and see the bigger impact of your decision. Goliath never stood a chance of defeating David. In fact, he was dead the moment David heard his voice shouting blasphemy against the Lord. That is because David came to the battlefield that day not thinking of himself, his mortality, fighting skill, or inability. He came fully focused on the Lord. These were *God's* people being intimidated by this monster, and David refused to stand aside and let God be mocked. David's thoughts were on how this victory would embolden his nation, and how it would strike fear into the hearts of their enemies. In short, David's eyes were on God's plan, not his own "qualifications." For those reasons, the story of David's victory over Goliath is still one of the most well-known Bible stories to this day.

The only way to walk in perseverance and endurance is trusting the Lord. Whether you're having an absolute blast or going through the worst time in your life, you have to trust the Lord. If you don't trust the Lord, the process is long and difficult. When you trust and have faith, the weight of worry, frustration, and fear fall off and the whole process becomes easier.

This does not mean that you need to put on a mask and act like you're not frustrated, worried, or afraid. Be real with the Lord. If you're upset, talk to Him about it. I run a community of houses for students from all over the world who have chosen to move to California. One year, we had one of the worst wildfire seasons in California history, where many people in our city lost their homes due to the fires. Right before that school year started, the owners of one of the houses I was subleasing called to let me know that they were evacuated from their home and needed a place to stay. They were not going to be renewing the lease with us because they needed to move into the property. We had everything ready to start the year and suddenly, I lost one of my larger properties.

This was not the first time we had been in need of housing on very short notice. God had always come through before, so there was not a doubt in my mind that we would get a house. It was most likely just going to happen last-minute. However, I was not satisfied with God moving at "11:59." I had to get real with the Lord. What I realized was that I was frustrated because my eyes were on me. He reminded me of a promise He had spoken to me before: "Your future is going to be great." As I got my eyes off of myself and onto Him and His promises for my life, the frustration lifted.

New houses were under construction in the same subdivision of the property I had just lost. All the properties had been reserved, and people were going to move in as soon as they were built. There was not a single available property. I randomly met the owner of a majority of the homes one day while looking at some other properties. Later, he called me and said he had reserved two properties that I could rent from him. I went from losing one property that was ten years old to getting two brand new properties larger than the one I had just lost for the same price! I am so thankful for God's faithfulness to work this situation out for good-for me and for the students living in the houses. He had a plan all along, and it came to pass once I brought my focus back onto Him.

When we see ourselves in Christ, we see ourselves as champions. Champions don't run from problems. When problems come up, you don't run from them–you run toward them and destroy them. When we see ourselves in Christ, we understand that we have been co-crucified, co-buried, co-raised, and co-seated. Now we're co-heirs with a commission to see His Kingdom come on earth.

We have to get to the place where when things come up, we say, "Okay, I'm going to destroy this thing." You have the Spirit of all truth who lives inside of you, and you have access to all things. So there is never a problem that you can't solve. Natural or supernatural, you have the solution!

God has a purpose and a plan for your life. The only prerequisite to the Gospel is that you believe it! You don't have to be exceptionally skilled. Think about it. What was Peter educated in? Fishing. Where did God call Peter? To the Jews, a people highly trained in the Law. What was Paul educated in? The Law. Yet, who did God call Paul to? The Gentiles. If He had called them according to their skill, then it would have been easy for them to boast in their own strength. But God called them to their weakness! In your weakness, He is strong. When you're weak in an area, stop complaining and grumbling. Start rejoicing that God is going to show up and show off through you!

Who Do You Remember?

I want you to take a look at this list and try to think of someone you know who has the same name.

- Shamua
- Shaphat
- Egal
- Caleb
- Gadiel
- Gadi
- Amiel
- Joshua
- Naphbai
- Gueil
- Palti
- Sether

Chances are there are only two names on this list that you recognize. If you know someone with a name other than Joshua or Caleb, you are in an extreme minority. These names are not made up or fictitious. They are the names of the ten spies that entered the Promised Land with Joshua and Caleb to discover what it was like.

There is a reason you probably know the names Joshua and Caleb but not Egal, Naphbai, or Sether. Of the twelve spies sent into the Promised Land, only two of them came back reporting that it was possible to take the land. Joshua and Caleb, alone among all the spies, believed God was able to work through them to give them victory. What did the others pay attention to? The giants, the fortified cities, how tough the other inhabitants looked, etc. In short, ten men saw problems and limitations while Joshua and Caleb saw God's power to overcome them.

What would have happened if those ten spies had come back with faith and trust in God? Chances are we'd still be naming our kids Gadi and Palti today. Why is that? Because history remembers those who were willing to take a stand, be bold, and trust in God. It remembers those among us who were undeterred by limitations and challenges, those who stood up, even though standing could have meant personal loss or even death.

Pastor Bill Johnson of Bethel Church once said, "If you live cautiously, your friends will call you wise. You just won't move many mountains." Mountains aren't moved by people who are satisfied with losing. Mountains are moved when people of faith decide that enough is enough. They are moved by people who decide that where they are isn't worth holding onto at the expense of what they could gain.

God is looking for people with that kind of faith. He is looking for those who are willing to say to a king, "God can deliver us, but even if He doesn't, we will not bow." He is waiting for those who will say to a giant, "This day the Lord will deliver you into my hand, and I will strike you and take your head from you." He is searching for those who stand up in the midst of a fearful congregation and say, "We are well able to defeat these giants and take the land. God has delivered them this day into our hands."

Perseverance may be a lost art, but it doesn't have to stay that way. There is a mighty move of God coming in the Body of Christ. He is coming to fill His people with hope, perseverance, and endurance. He is coming to transform us into radical, bold, sold-out followers of Jesus, who are unwilling to yield or bow to fear and disappointment. He desires for you to be counted among those who shaped history and changed a nation's destiny. If you let Him do His work in you, you will never be the same. Will you say yes?

"For we were saved in this hope, but hope that is seen is not hope; for why does one still hope for what he sees? But if we hope for what we do not see, we eagerly wait for it with perseverance."

–Romans 8:24-25

Additional Resources

The Lost Art of Discipleship

God's Model for Transforming the World

Discipleship is not a man-made idea. It is God's design for world transformation. *The Lost Art of Discipleship* is the uncovering of Heaven's blueprints for remodeling the kingdoms of the earth into the Kingdom of our God. In his cornerstone book, Daniel Newton pulls from 20 years of experience in discipleship. As you read, prepare your heart to be ignited with the fires of revival that once swept the globe as in the days of the Early Church. It is time for the people of God to arise and shine, for our light has come!

Available at GracePlaceMedia.com

@GracePlaceDiscipleship

Additional Resources

The Lost Art of Discipleship

Workbook

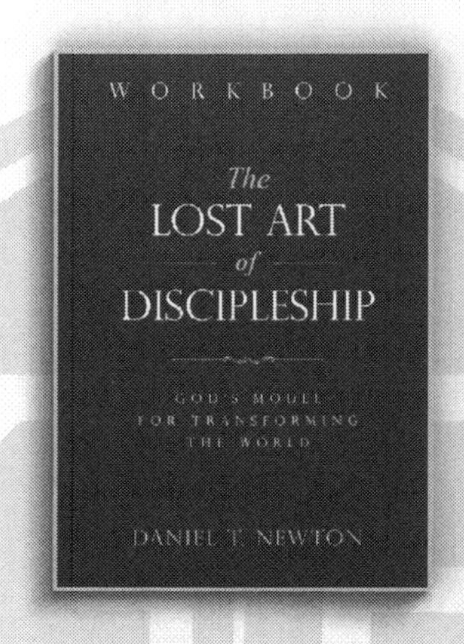

Enrich your understanding and increase your mastery of God's model for world transformation. This companion manual to *The Lost Art of Discipleship* book is filled with exclusive additional content, in-depth exercises, and practical coaching to introduce a lifestyle of discipleship in your day-to-day walk. Whether you have been following the Lord for years or recently surrendered your life to Jesus, this manual breaks down the Great Commission and equips you for a life of fruitfulness!

Additional Resources

The Lost Art of Discipleship

Online Course

You can live the Great Commission. Every believer is called to embrace Jesus' final command: to make disciples... and this interactive online course is designed to take you even deeper into the rich content taught in The Lost Art of Discipleship.

Whether you are wanting to position yourself as a son or daughter, lead as a father or mother, or create a culture of discipleship, this school is for you! Rediscover the lost art with over five hours of video content, practical teaching, quizzes, and supernatural activations from Daniel Newton.

Additional Resources

Truth in Tension
55 Days to Living
in Balance

Never Give Up
The Supernatural Power of
Christ-like Endurance

Other Titles

It Is Finished
Exposing the Conquered Giants of
Fear, Pride, and Condemnation

All Things
Have Become New, Work Together
for Good, and Are Possible

Available at GracePlaceMedia.com

@GracePlaceDiscipleship

Additional Resources

Immeasurable

Reviewing the Goodness of God

You are made in the image of the Miracle Worker, designed to manifest His glorious nature. *Immeasurable: Reviewing the Goodness of God* is a collection of 100 real-life stories of salvation, healing, deliverance, signs and wonders, reconciliation, and provision. Every miracle is a prophetic declaration of what God wants to do in, through, and for someone just like you.

Additional Resources

GP Music: Beginnings

Grace Place Ministries'
Debut Worship Album

Everyone has a story. Most people don't realize that God doesn't just want to improve their story. He wants to rewrite it. *Beginnings* offers a fresh start, a new focus. This worship album invites you into the core anthems of grace and truth which have impacted us at Grace Place.

Our prayer is that this album helps you lay down your past mistakes, your present circumstances, and your future worries in order to lift both hands high in surrender to the One you were created to worship. We ask that you join us in a new beginning—an exciting start to a life filled with perseverance, focus, and surrender.

Available on all music platforms
or at GracePlaceMedia.com

@GracePlaceDiscipleship